Fireworks

and

Song of the Nightingale

in Full Score

Igor Stravinsky

DOVER PUBLICATIONS, INC.
Mineola, New York

Bibliographical Note

This Dover edition, first published in 2000, is a new compilation of two works originally published separately. B. Schott's Söhne, Mainz, originally published *Feu d'Artifice: Une Fantaisie pour Grand Orchestre, Op. 4,* [1910]. Edition Russe de Musique, Berlin, originally published *Chant du Rossignol: Poème Symphonique pour Orchestre,* 1921.

We are grateful to composer David L. Post and to The Sibley Music Library, Eastman School of Music, for the loan of these authoritative early editions.

Stanley Appelbaum's prefatory notes were written specially for this edition. The glossary is newly added. Errata listed separately in the original *Rossignol* edition have been incorporated into the music without comment.

International Standard Book Number: 0-486-41392-6

Manufactured in the United States of America
Dover Publications, Inc., 31 East 2nd Street, Mineola, N.Y. 11501

CONTENTS

Introduction

The two entertaining, virtuosic orchestral works by Igor Stravinsky (1882–1971) included in this volume were first published eleven years apart, yet they were virtually contemporary in their inception. They both go back ultimately to the second half of the first decade of the twentieth century, when the composer finally considered that his student days were over, and when he was beginning to assign opus numbers to his works.

Fireworks (Op. 4)

From 1902 until his death in June 1908, Nikolai Rimsky-Korsakov was Stravinsky's private teacher and mentor in St. Petersburg. *Fireworks* (in Russian, *Féyerverk* [a loan word from German]; in French, *Feu d'artifice*) was planned as a wedding gift for Rimsky's daughter Nadezhda.[1] Even the most serious biographers of Stravinsky, variously interpreting the tiniest clues, are in dispute about the time of composition and the date of early performances. The most recent and reasonable view dates the composition to the spring or early summer of 1908; other views take it up to as much as a year later. It was written at Ustilug, a northwestern Ukrainian village where the family owned an estate. The official premiere was at a Siloti[2] concert in St. Petersburg on January 9, 1910 (one historian places it almost a year earlier), but *Fireworks* had already been performed some three times at private concerts in 1909. The one attended by the impresario Serge Diaghilev (1872–1929), who was presenting Russian operas and ballets in Paris, may have been the one at the Conservatory. At any rate, it was still in 1909, because Diaghilev, instantly attuned to Stravinsky's genius for orchestration and for propulsive, danceable music, signed him up in that year—first merely to orchestrate piano works by Grieg and Chopin, but eventually assigning him to set the preexisting scenario for *The Firebird*. That ballet, premiered in Paris in 1910, established the composer's international reputation. In October 1909 the conductor Siloti recommended *Fireworks* to the publisher B. Schott's Söhne in Mainz, who published the full score in 1910.

Before writing *Fireworks,* Stravinsky had completed his Symphony No. 1 in E-flat Major, Op. 1 (composed between 1905 and 1907), of which the Scherzo was the most successful movement, and the *Scherzo fantastique,* Op. 3 (composed between June 1907 and March 1908). *Fireworks* is yet another such *moto perpetuo* scherzo, perky and bubbly. Brief as it is (playing time is between 3 and 4 minutes), it includes a notable calmer interlude that is immediately reminiscent of one of the major themes of Dukas's *Sorcerer's Apprentice* (1897), though Stravinsky's music is more ethereal and harmonically emancipated.[3]

In 1917 Diaghilev staged the work in Rome as a sort of *son et lumière* spectacle with constructions and lighting by the eminent Futurist painter Giacomo Balla (1871–1958). Stravinsky often included this engaging orchestral piece in concerts he himself conducted. It was natural for him to perform it during his triumphant return to St. Petersburg (then still Leningrad) in 1962—but Nadezhda Steinberg declined her special invitation. There had never been much love lost between Stravinsky and the dedicatees of *Fireworks.*

Song of the Nightingale

Though this tone poem is completely self-sufficient, and can be enjoyed on its own, it *is* derived from an earlier Stravinsky work (the opera *The Nightingale*), and its three printed subheadings ("Chinese March," "Song of the Nightingale," and "Performance by the Mechanical Nightingale") make it abundantly clear that we are dealing with program music. So that some words about its program will not be out of place.

The opera, *The Nightingale* (in Russian, *Solovéy;* in French, *Le rossignol*), is based on the famous fairy tale of the same name (in Danish, *Nattergalen*) by Hans Christian Andersen (1805–1875), written in 1844 and said to be inspired by a hopeless love for the coloratura soprano Jenny Lind (1820–1887), the "Swedish nightingale." A typical Andersen mix of satire and sentimentality, "The Nightingale" teaches that human warmth is better than wealth, that bureaucrats are divorced from Nature and the things that are truly worthwhile, and that great art can dwell within a very plain exterior (the Ugly Duckling theme). The Emperor of China reads in a foreign book that his grandest possession is an amazingly musical nightingale that lives very near his palace. Surprised, he sends his courtiers to invite it to sing for him. When it does, he is moved to tears, which is all the reward the bird desires. The bird is confined to the court, enjoying a popularity that becomes exaggerated, until Japanese envoys bring a mechanical nightingale as a gift to the Emperor. It is a sensation, though it can perform only one song. The live bird, finding itself unappreciated, escapes, and in his pique the Emperor exiles it. Five years later, when the Emperor is mortally ill and the mechanical bird is broken, the real nightingale returns voluntarily, refreshing the Emperor with its song and driving away Death and his specters. The

---

[1] In 1908 she married the composer Maximilian Oseyevich Steinberg (Shteynberg; 1883–1946), who became Rimsky's musical executor. His own works were based largely on folk themes. As a teacher, his students included Shostakovich.

[2] Siloti (Alexander Ilyich Ziloti; 1863–1945) was a pianist (a pupil of Liszt) and a conductor who, with his own orchestra, championed new music from 1903 to the Revolution. Later, he taught at Juilliard from 1924 to 1942.

[3] A lengthy musical analysis of *Fireworks* (and of the opera *The Nightingale*) can be found in Richard Taruskin's *Stravinsky and the Russian Traditions: A Biography of the Works Through "Mavra,"* University of California Press, Berkeley, 1996 (2 vols.).

bird promises to visit the Emperor often, though it refuses to be tied down. When the courtiers enter, expecting to find the Emperor dead, he greets them cheerfully.

Stravinsky collaborated on the (Russian) libretto with a friend from the Rimsky-Korsakov circle, Stepan Stepanovich Mitusov[4] (1878–1942). Work probably began late in 1907; by early 1908, the whole thing had been sketchily planned, and the first act had been written out. The plan was for three brief acts (so brief that they are really three scenes of a one-act opera). The librettists hewed very close to the Andersen story, retaining a large number of amusing details, but telescoping the total time of the events. Their main innovation was to take a character whom Andersen mentions only fleetingly at the outset of his story, a fisherman who appreciates the nightingale's singing, and to give him the second largest singing role, with an extended opening number and a sort of "Greek chorus" commentary at the end of each act. Their three acts skillfully break the story down into three different locales: the seaside forest in which the courtiers, sent by the Emperor, find the bird and invite it to the palace; the throne room, in which preparations for the reception take place in silhouette ("Chinese shadows") behind a gauze curtain, and subsequently the Emperor arrives, the nightingale performs, the Japanese envoys come, the mechanical bird does its turn, and the real one escapes; and the Emperor's bedroom, where the real bird returns to drive away Death, and the courtiers enter to find the Emperor cured.

With only the first-act text finished, Stravinsky began composing in the autumn of 1908, continuing into 1909 (most of the task was done at the Ustilug estate, with Stravinsky composing directly in full score). The music of this first act is romantic and rich, with many reminiscences of Russian composers of the preceding generation, leavened by the influence of Debussy and other French moderns. (Much of the word setting, especially when the work is performed in French,[5] is surprisingly like a "flash forward" to Poulenc.) Stravinsky and Mitusov went no further in 1909, because the composer suddenly received so many assignments from Diaghilev for Paris. *The Firebird* was produced in 1910; *Petrushka*, in 1911; and *The Rite of Spring* in 1913. By then Stravinsky was a new person, both financially and artistically.

In 1913, a new Moscow theatrical venture, the Free Theatre (Svobodny Teatr), asked Stravinsky to complete his opera in time for their 1914 season. Stravinsky, who was then immersed in ballet composition, and whose compositional style had made incredible advances since he wrote the first act of the opera, was hesitant and suggested that they produce the first act as à permanent fragment (he was also

willing to publish it that way); but he found it hard to resist the big fee that the Free Theatre was offering for the complete opera. Fortunately for Stravinsky, Diaghilev had an option on the venture, because the Free Theatre folded before much time had elapsed but Diaghilev was fully prepared to undertake the premiere. Stravinsky adamantly refused to revise the first act; in the face of his fears that the work might be too hybrid, because he could no longer revert to his 1908/1909 style, he rationalized that the first act depicted unspoiled nature, whereas the two remaining acts would take place in the hypercivilized, "overheated" imperial palace.

The libretto for Acts Two and Three was still to be written out. Mitusov visited Stravinsky at Ustilug in the summer of 1913, and Stravinsky visited Mitusov in Warsaw on his way back to Western Europe in the fall. Composition was done in 1913 and 1914 at Ustilug and in two of the French Swiss towns in which Stravinsky resided, Clarens and Leysin (the former on, the latter close to, the eastern end of the Lake of Geneva). The work inevitably did turn out to be a hybrid (though time has considerably softened the contrast), the music of the second act being *brillante,* dashing, witty, virtuosic, and more in the nature of a pageant, while the third act is once again lyrical, but in a much more advanced way than Act One.

Diaghilev's production was subsidized by Sir Joseph Beecham, music-loving pharmaceuticals manufacturer and father of the conductor Thomas Beecham; Sir Joseph had undertaken to finance Diaghilev's 1914 season at Drury Lane, where *The Nightingale* was to be performed—but after its premiere in Paris. The first performance was at the Opéra on May 26, 1914, in Russian, with Pierre Monteux conducting (he had already conducted the premieres of *Petrushka* and *The Rite of Spring*), with sets and costumes by Alexandre Benois, and with choreography by Boris Romanov. The singers of the Nightingale's and Fisherman's roles were placed in the orchestra, and there was a lot of miming onstage. The opera was well received, but so relatively tamely that Stravinsky sorely missed the pandemonium that the *Rite of Spring* premiere had aroused. Truly, his heart was no longer in opera at that particular time.

The opera full score was published in 1923 by the Edition Russe de Musique, the Parisian agency of the Berlin house Russischer Musik Verlag, which had been founded in 1909 by the conductor Serge Koussevitsky (1874–1951). The opera is not very often performed, largely because of its modest length (playing time of 45 to 50 minutes), which necessitates a split bill (usually shared with ballets). In 1962, Stravinsky "revised" the opera, chiefly altering a number of metronome markings.

In 1916 Diaghilev or Stravinsky (accounts differ) had the idea of converting the opera into a more fashionable and profitable ballet. Diaghilev drew up a letter of agreement that was remarkable for its precise instructions on which parts of the opera to include and exclude. Stravinsky followed these guidelines by and large, but not slavishly. At some early point the composer provided a rough scenario, containing three scenes that corresponded to Acts Two and Three of the opera (the then old-fashioned Act One was to be totally abandoned): "The Fête in the Palace" (extending through the end of the "Marche chinoise," the Emperor's entrance procession), "The Two Nightingales" (real and mechanical songs, extending through the end of the origi-

---

[4]Also transliterated as Mitussov, Mitousov, etc. (Almost every Russian name is susceptible of varying transliterations; in the present Introduction [with a couple of exceptions] only the version most familiar to Americans is used. The transliteration here of the Russian titles of musical works is also informal, not scientific.) Mitusov stayed in Russia after the Revolution and became a choral conductor.

[5]The French translation, made when the opera was finally completed, was by the music critic and historian Mikhail Dmitri Calvocoressi (1877–1944), a friend of Stravinsky's (he also translated some of the composer's Russian songs).

nal second act), and "The Illness and Recovery of the Emperor" (the original third act). (These do not represent hard-and-fast musical divisions of the completed ballet/tone poem, which plays without other breaks than an occasional brief general pause or fermata.)

Stravinsky completed the conversion at Morges, on the Lake of Geneva, on April 4, 1917, but the music was not to be performed for over two and a half years, and a concert performance preceded the theatrical premiere. (The new work was called *Song of the Nightingale*; in Russian, *Pésnya solov'yá*; in French, *Chant du rossignol.*) Diaghilev had tried to present the ballet sooner; flirting with the Italian Futurists in 1917 (cf. the *Fireworks* production designed by Balla), he commissioned the sets and costumes from the then still young and impecunious artist Fortunato Depero (1892–1960), but Depero's sets were sold off piecemeal by his landlady to recoup her back rent! Ernest Ansermet, already associated with Diaghilev and Stravinsky for some years, performed the new music for the first time with his recently formed Orchestre de la Suisse Romande (French Switzerland) at the Victoria Hall in Geneva on December 6, 1919. The audience, not yet familiar with the "audacities" that Paris had been exposed to for years, reacted badly, but Stravinsky was very pleased with the performance, concluding that his music was better served in a concert hall, after plenty of rehearsals, than in the rough and tumble of a seething theater, with all the variables that can affect a performance.

Ansermet was also the conductor at the premiere of the ballet, which took place at the Paris Opéra on February 2, 1920. The great Tamara Karsavina danced the part of the Nightingale, while the sets and costumes were signed by no less a luminary than Henri Matisse. The relative failure of the ballet has often been laid to the charge of the famous choreographer Léonide Massine (Myasin), who intentionally divorced the footwork from the musical beat, leading the audience to believe that the dancers were at fault. Stravinsky, always self-serving, later claimed that *Song of the Nightingale* had been conceived (by himself alone) strictly as a "symphonic poem" and that he had been sidetracked into the ballet production. When the full score of the work was published in 1921, by the Edition Russe de Musique, not only were there no stage directions; there wasn't the slightest hint of the tawdry balletic past of the piece. Yet its stage days, though limited, were not over. Diaghilev revived the work in 1925, assigning the choreography to his newcomer, George Balanchine; the Nightingale was danced by the fifteen-year-old Alicia Markova; again, various contretemps militated against success. In 1972, when the New York City Ballet was staging everything imaginable of Stravinsky's in a huge festival commemorating the ninetieth anniversary of his birth, *Song of the Nightingale* had another day in the sun; the choreographer was John Taras, the Nightingale was Gelsey Kirkland, the designer was Rouben Ter-Arutunian.

From this point on, we shall discuss *Song of the Nightingale* strictly as a tone poem, though not forgetting the opera from which it was derived (*The Nightingale*). The tone poem, with its 20 minutes or so of playing time, is less than half the length of the opera, which is understandable, considering that it doesn't use the first act of the opera. The above-mentioned three printed subheads in the score do *not* represent new "movements"; they indicate outstanding

tours de force that are self-contained (the Chinese March has sometimes been performed on its own at concerts) but do not hold up the overall flow of the music. The orchestra is somewhat smaller than that required by the opera (only two players instead of three for each woodwind instrument, for example), and there are more solos and small "ensembles" (concertante groupings), often giving a chamber effect within the general full texture. Both the reduction of instrumental forces and this less massive use of the orchestra were in line with Stravinsky's new tendencies in the late 1910s and early 1920s (cf. his experiments in *Histoire du soldat* and *Les noces,* to name just two outstanding works of those years). A distinctive feature of *Song of the Nightingale* is the occasional use of solo instruments to render vocal lines from the opera: the Nightingale's arias are represented by a solo flute and/or a solo violin; the Fisherman's songs, by a solo trumpet.

The following rough breakdown of *Song of the Nightingale* vis-à-vis the original opera (Acts Two and Three only!) intentionally disregards small additions and excisions, differences in pitch and key, changes in instrumentation, and similar secondary features.[6]

Measure 1 up to just before rehearsal number [13]: this scurrying music corresponds to the opening of Act Two of the opera, the silhouetted scene behind a scrim in which the Emperor's court functionaries prepare for his arrival to hear the nightingale for the first time.

[13] to just before [16]: new music, representing the nightingale, in place of a small part of the original silhouetted scene.

[16] to just before [18]: corresponds to the original conclusion of the silhouetted scene.

[18] to just before [37]: "Chinese March"; the entrance of the Emperor and his dignitaries.

[37] to just before [38]: a short bridge replacing original sung dialogue.

[38] to just before [44]: "Song of the Nightingale," incorporating not only music sung by the nightingale to the Emperor at this point of Act Two of the opera, but also some thematic material from its song to Death in Act Three.

[44] to just before [55]: A varied recapitulation of the opening, scurrying, scrim music; this does *not* occur in the opera, but is a new feature of the instrumental version which helps to bind it together in its own new terms.

[55] to just before [58]: corresponds to some of the music of the Japanese envoys who bring the mechanical nightingale.

[58] to just before [61]: "Performance by the Mechanical Nightingale."

[61] to just before [68]: corresponds to most of the remaining dialogue of Act Two, concerning the escape of the real nightingale, its banishment, and the Emperor's departure from the throne room.

[6]Note: it is clear from the original 1920 reviews of the ballet that there was music preceding the opening of the music as published in 1921 (and as performed in the concert hall ever since): a sort of prelude made use of the Fisherman's first song from Act One of the opera. This prelude is said to have been used in some subsequent performances of the ballet.

68 to just before 71: the Fisherman's commentary on events (trumpet solo); end of original Act Two of opera.

71 to just before 80: corresponds to the original instrumental prelude to Act Three, in which the Emperor is on his death bed.

80 to just before 92: the return of the real nightingale, its songs to the Emperor and to Death (who departs), the recovery of the Emperor, the nightingale's promise to keep in touch. (This section is especially heavily abridged and altered from the operatic version.)

92 to just before 96: funeral march of the courtiers, cheerful greeting by the Emperor (the last three harp chords on page 116 and the first one on page 117 correspond to the words "Bonjour à tous" in the French libretto).

96 to end: the Fisherman's concluding song (trumpet solo).

The discerning critic Eric Walter White is surely too hard on *Song of the Nightingale* when he emphasizes that it was "not really symphonic in intention" and dismisses it as a "pleasant orchestral reminder of some of the lyrical delights that are to be found in the opera." Actually, it is more successful as an instrumental work than *The Nightingale* was as an opera (because of the opera's hybrid styles, impossibility of showing the main character on stage, imbalance of pageant over vocalism); and the far-reaching and deep-seated changes that Stravinsky made qualify it as a thoroughly autonomous independent piece (though, as the writer of this Introduction obviously believes, the listener's knowledge of its antecedents can only serve to enhance his pleasure).

Stanley Appelbaum

GLOSSARY OF FRENCH TERMS
IN THE MUSIC

avec un morceau de fil de fer, with a piece of wire [for triangle]

baguette dure, hard stick [for percussion]
bouché, "stopped" note(s) [for horn]

"Chant du rossignol," "Song of the nightingale" [subhead, p. 72]
comme un écho, like an echo

encore plus calme, still calmer
en dehors, prominent, bring out
étouffez (subitement), damp [the sound] (quickly) [for triangle, harp]

"Jeu du rossignol mécanique," "Performance by the mechanical
 nightingale" [subhead, p. 88]

les pavillons en l'air jusqu'au signe . . . , the bells [of the horns] in the air
 until the sign . . .

"Marche chinoise," "Chinese march" [subhead, p. 52]

m.d. [main droite], right hand
m.g. [main gauche], left hand

ordinairement, in the usual way [cancels previous playing instruction]
ouvert, open [for brass]

pour l'oreille, literally, "for the ear"—the actual sound of a string harmonic
préparez le Si♭ (etc.), prepare [tune to] the B♭ (etc.) [for harp]
près de la table, [play] close to the sounding board [for harp]

sons étouffés, damped sounds [for harp]

toutes les croches sont égales, all 8ths are equal
très en dehors, very prominent
très serré, very tight, compact [for string tremolo]

FOOTNOTE, p. 113:
Pour obtenir cette note il faut introduire un cornet de carton souple
dans le pavillon de l'instrument.

> To produce this pitch, the player must insert a cone of pliable cardboard
> in the bell of the instrument. [for clarinet]

To N. and M. Steinberg

Fireworks

A Fantasy for Large Orchestra

Feu d'Artifice: Une Fantaisie pour Grand Orchestre

Op. 4 (1908)

INSTRUMENTATION

Piccolo [Flauto piccolo, Fl. picc.]
2 Flutes [Flauti grandi, Fl.]
2 Oboes [Oboi]
    Ob. II doubles English Horn [C. Ingl.]
3 Clarinets in A [Clarinetti, Cl.]
    Cl. III doubles Bass Clarinet [Cl. basso]
2 Bassoons [Fagotti, Fag., Fg.]

6 Horns in F [Corni, Cor.]
3 Trumpets in A [Trombe, Tr.]
3 Tenor Trombones [Tromboni tenori, Tromb.]
Tuba

Timpani [Timp.]

Percussion
    Triangle [Triangolo, Triang.]
    Cymbals [Piatti]
    Bass Drum [Gr(an) Cassa]

Celesta
Bells [Campanelli, Camp(l).]
2 Harps [Arpa]

Violin I   (16)   [Violini, Viol.]
Violin II   (14)   [Violini, Viol.]
Violas   (12)   [Viole]
Cellos   (10)   [Violoncelli, Vcl.]
Basses   (8)   [Contrabbassi]

Triangolo.

Piatti.

Song of the Nightingale

Symphonic Poem for Orchestra

Chant du Rossignol: Poème Symphonique pour Orchestre

Arranged and orchestrated, 1917, from *Le Rossignol,*
a musical fairy tale after Hans Christian Andersen, composed 1908–14

INSTRUMENTATION

2 Flutes [Flauto grande, Fl. gr.]
  Fl. II doubles Piccolo [Flauto piccolo, Fl. picc.]
2 Oboes [Oboi]
  Ob. II doubles English Horn [Cor. ingl.]
2 Clarinets in A & B♭ [Clarinetto in La/Si♭, Clar.]
  Cl. II doubles E♭ Clarinet [Clarinetto piccolo (Mi♭), Clar. picc.]
2 Bassoons [Fagotti, Fag.]

4 Horns in F [Corni]
3 Trumpets in C [Trombe, Trbe/a]
3 Trombones [Tromboni, Trboni/e]
Tuba

Timpani

Percussion
  Triangle [Triangolo, Trg.]
  Tambourine [Tambour de Basque, Tamb. de B.]
  Cymbals [Piatti]
  Snare Drum [Caisse claire, Csse. cl.]
  Field Drum (or Snare Drum) [Tamburo (militaire), Tamb. mil.]
  Bass Drum [Gr(an) C(assa)]
  Tam-tam

Celesta
Piano
2 Harps [Arpa]

Violin I, II [Violini, V-ni]
Violas [Viole, V-le]
Cellos [(Violoncelli), V-c.]
Basses [(Contrabbassi), C-B.]

Igor Strawinsky

Chant du Rossignol
poème symphonique pour orchestre

Игорь Стравинскій
симфоническая поэма для оркестра

37

Marche chinoise   Китайскій маршъ

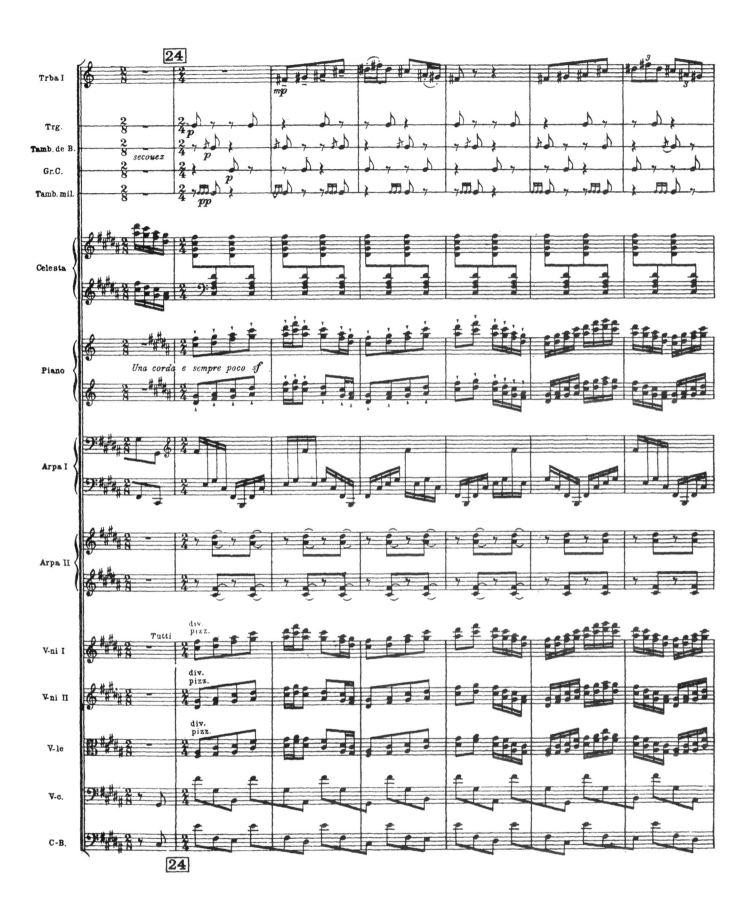

Chant du Rossignol

Пѣсня соловья

Jeu du rossignol
mécanique

Игра искусственнаго
Соловья

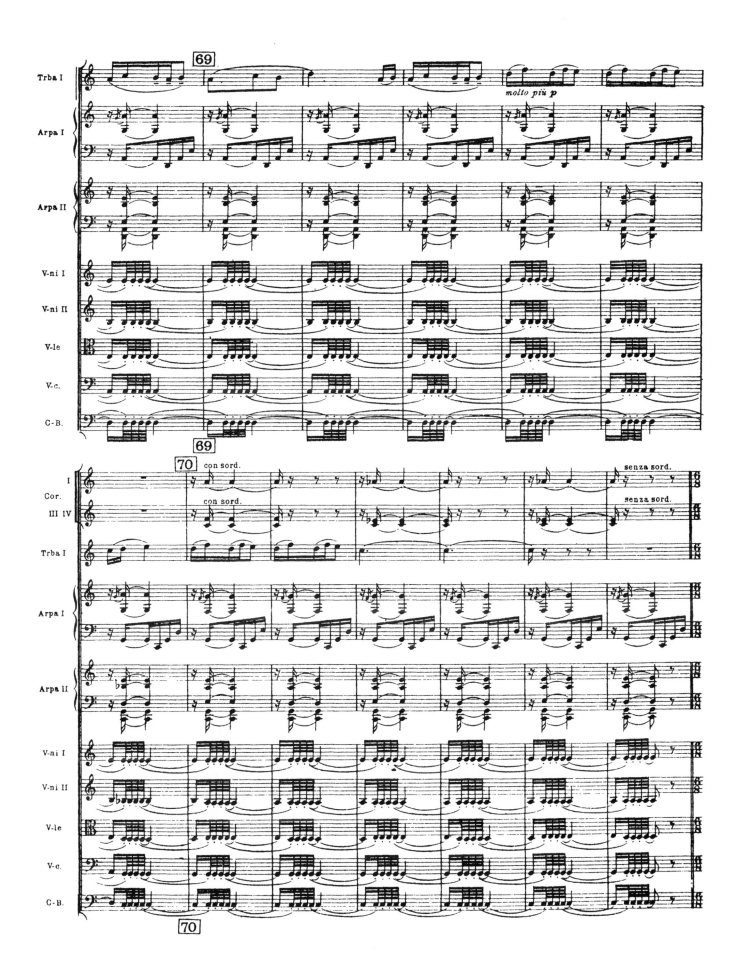

*) pizz. *glissando* sul Re

*) Pour obtenir cette note il faut introduire un cornet de carton souple dans le pavillon de l'instrument.

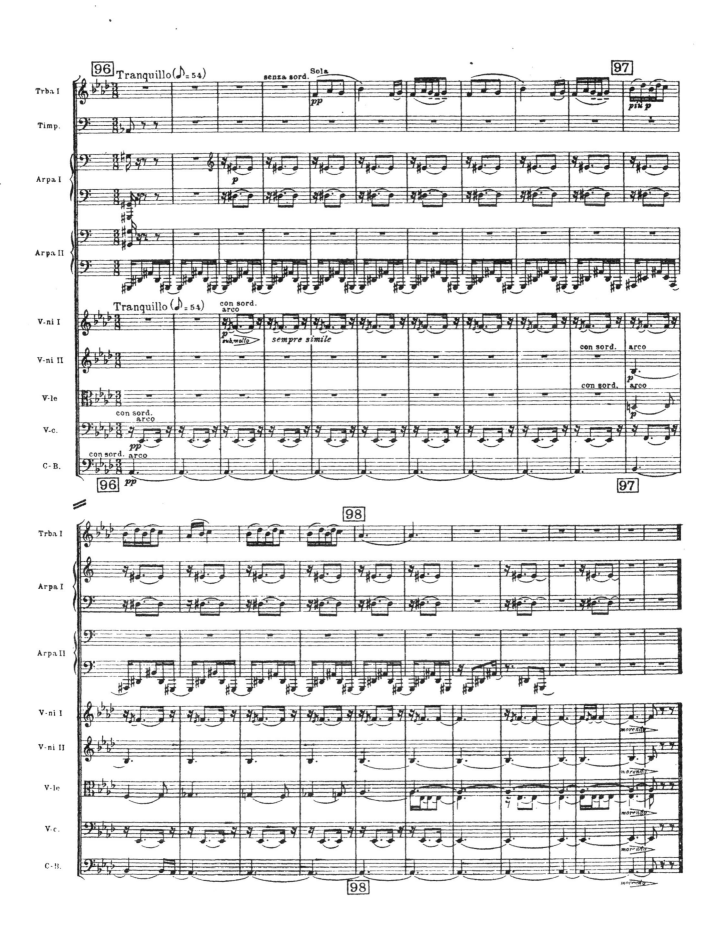

END OF EDITION